Sometimes, the best leadership lessons come from the least likely of sources.

There are messages all around you – ones that can help improve both the way you lead and the results you achieve.

Your challenge: Pay attention, listen, learn ... and APPLY.

The  Company

To order additional copies of this handbook or for information on other WALK THE TALK® products and services, contact us at
1.888.822.9255
or visit our website at
www.walkthetalk.com

"MEMOS" To: Managers

©2002 David Cottrell and Performance Systems Corporation. All rights reserved.
No part of this book may be reproduced in any form without written permission from the publisher. International rights and foreign translations are available only through negotiation of a licensing agreement with the publisher.

Inquiries regarding permission for use of the material contained in this book should be addressed to:

    The WALK THE TALK Company
    2925 LBJ Freeway, Suite 201
    Dallas, Texas 75234
    972.243.8863

WALK THE TALK books may be purchased for educational, business, or sales promotion use.

WALK THE TALK® and The WALK THE TALK® Company are registered trademarks of Performance Systems Corporation.

All characters, organizations, and events portrayed in this handbook are fictitious. Any resemblance to actual people, names, organizations, logos, or events is purely coincidental.

Printed in the United States of America
10 9 8 7 6 5 4 3 2 1

Edited by Melissa Ventura
Printed by The Graphics Group

This book is printed on recycled paper.

ISBN 1-885228-45-7

David Cottrell and Eric Harvey

Leadership Lessons to Read, Learn From, and Apply

Introduction Memo

TO: Leaders at All Levels

FROM: David Cottrell and Eric Harvey

DATE: Today

SUBJECT: **"MEMOS" To: Managers**

Would you like to know what your employees are REALLY thinking and feeling ... or hear what is being whispered when you are not around? Imagine what you and other leaders would learn if you could receive totally candid feedback from your teams and your colleagues. Just think how you'd be able to improve your leadership effectiveness if only you could be a fly on the wall – learning what to do, and what not to do, from the information (obvious and hidden) that's all around you.

Ever wish you could climb inside peoples' heads and get a first-hand feel for how they perceive your organization, its leadership, and you? **You're about to do just that!**

"MEMOS" To: Managers is a unique and powerful resource that provides information which is usually difficult to acquire. It allows you to experience leadership – both good and bad – through the eyes of others. And it does so in a straight talk, no-holds-barred way.

Some of the learning will be subtle – some will be "in your face." And all of it is based on our personal observations and real-world experiences over many years.

You'll find that several of the "memos" come from unique places: written on walls, a voice mail left on a corporate hot-line, e-mails to co-workers and spouses, speech notes left on a podium, and even a conversation at the "proverbial water cooler." And there's a bunch that come from more standard forms of written communication.

Regardless of the source, each item contains an important message ... and a significant key learning point. Your challenge is to absorb the learning, and then APPLY it to, and through, your leadership behaviors.

Perhaps the most important reason that **"MEMOS" To: Managers** should be part of your leadership toolbox is because the messages are from employees at all levels ... just like the people you work with every day.

So read on, pay attention, and make the most of what you experience!

Table of Contents

A Crumpled piece of paper left on a manager's desk ... 7
A letter to a previous manager ... 8
Training class exercise results - Parts 1, 2, and 3 ... 9-11
Meeting evaluations - by manager and staff member ... 12-13
Graffiti found on restroom wall ... 14
New criteria for the "Manager of the Year" award ... 15
Conversation around "the proverbial water cooler" ... 16-17
E-mail sent to a recently promoted co-worker ... 18
Meeting agenda with participant's margin notes ... 19
An employee's self-commendation ... 20
Three e-mails sent home by a traveling spouse ... 21-23
Leadership survey results - Cover memo and summary ... 24-25
Letter to the Editor of the in-house newsletter ... 26
E-mail typed out of frustration but never sent ... 27
"T-shirt Exercise" from manager/employee training ... 28-29
More restroom graffiti ... 30
Voice mail left on the "ethics hotline" ... 31
A week in the life of a manager who "walks the talk" ... 32-33
The resignation - Parts 1, 2, 3 and 4 ... 34-37
Results of employee training table group exercise ... 38
Bulletin boards from very different organizations ... 39-41
Retirement speech notes left on podium ... 42-43
Memo to file: Key learning from "MEMOS" To: Managers ... 44-45

A crumpled piece of paper found somewhere and anonymously left on a manager's desk ...

A letter to a previous manager ...

THE TECHNOLOGY GROUP

Dear Andy,

Recently, I took over managing the team that you led before your promotion. I knew that I had some big shoes to fill, but I had no idea how BIG those shoes really were. You were definitely a positive influence on this group!

At one of our first meetings, I asked team members "What made Andy so successful as a leader?" I thought that you might be interested in their comments.

While there were many different reasons cited, something very unusual happened – every person's list included the same three characteristics! I've tried this same exercise with other teams in the past, and rarely have I seen such a consistency in responses.

The three characteristics that every person mentioned were:

1) You are an outstanding motivator who gives recognition where and when deserved.
2) You are a great coach – you take the time to develop your staff.
3) You are a person of high integrity who "walks the talk."

Wow! That's an impressive list. And a lot of other great stuff was also mentioned – like how well you communicated, solved problems, listened, accepted responsibility, and exhibited positive leadership ... even when times were tough.

Andy, you are one terrific leader. I'm honored to follow in your footsteps ... and to "inherit" such a terrific group.

Best wishes in your new assignment,

DJ

Training class exercise – Part 1 of 3: Memo from Training Director to Managers ...

Internal Correspondence

To: All Managers
From: Director of Training
Subject: Leadership

One of the directives for the Training Department this year is to provide feedback to management on our employees' perception of leadership here at TreeView.

During the past several weeks, over two hundred employees – representing every division and functional area of our City – have participated in various training programs at our municipal headquarters.

While in training, each employee was asked to complete two sentences:

1. I do my best work for bosses who ...
2. I am least effective when working for bosses who are ...

The feedback was anonymous, and each employee could include up to five responses per sentence.

Attached are the twenty most common responses for each sentence. Notice that, according to our employees, "people skills" can be either the greatest contributor or the greatest detriment to our leadership success.

I recommend you consider replicating this same exercise within your teams – and apply the key learning.

Training class exercise - Part 2 of 3: First attachment to the Training Director's memo ...

I do my best work for bosses who ...

Treat me with respect.
Listen to my ideas.
Keep me informed about what is going on.
I trust.
Are considerate of my time.
Provide feedback on how I am doing.
Take the time to train me to do my job well.
Support diversity.
Display enthusiasm.
Hire good people for me to work with.
Are ethical.
Encourage me to become the best.
Lead by example.
Balance work and home.
Make work enjoyable.
Are good coaches.
Clearly define expectations.
Handle pressure and disappointment well.
Perform with integrity.
Recognize me for doing a good job.

Training class exercise - Part 3 of 3: Second attachment to the Training Director's memo ...

I am least effective when working for bosses who are ...

Negative and cynical.
Unwilling to share credit for successes.
Inflexible.
Slow on the recognition but quick on the blame.
Insensitive.
Dishonest and unethical.
Critical of upper management.
Consistently late for meetings.
Reluctant to share important information.
Indecisive and afraid to address problems.
Disrespectful of others' time.
Hypocritical.
More interested in politics than people.
Empire builders.
Resistant to change.
Unwilling to deal with "bad news."
Never wrong.
Unfair and inconsistent.

Recent meeting evaluation - Completed by the manager ...

ABC Enterprises
Meeting Evaluation

1. Meeting Description (topic, date, etc.): _____
   Sept. 4th
   Quality meeting to set fiscal
   year goals

2. On a scale of 1 to 10, how would you rate this meeting? (circle one number)

   1   2   3   4   5   6   7   8   **9**   10
   Awful   Acceptable   Outstanding

   Why? _could have had more participation, but when people agree ... they agree!_

3. Suggestions for future meetings: _____
   think the meeting went very well

4. Name: _T.R. Franklin_   Date: _09/04_
   (optional)

> Evaluation of the same meeting – Completed by a staff member ...

ABC Enterprises
Meeting Evaluation

1. Meeting Description (topic, date, etc.): _____
   Department quality meeting on Sept. 4th

2. On a scale of 1 to 10, how would you rate this meeting? (circle one number)

   1 **(2)** 3 4 5 6 7 8 9 10
   Awful   Acceptable   Outstanding

   Why? _Preach, preach, preach! We know quality is important but need to develop more how-to techniques_

3. Suggestions for future meetings: _____
   Ask US for ideas ... we don't check our brains at the front door you know!

4. Name: _____ Date: _Sept. 8th_
         (optional)

Graffiti found on restroom wall ...

roses are red
employees are blue
bust your ~~CENSORED~~
and they still ignore you!

Memo from CEO outlining new criteria for the "Manager of the Year" award ...

To: All Managers
From: CEO
Subject: NEW CRITERIA FOR "THE EAGLE"

From my perspective, one of the most significant recognition awards we have in our organization is THE EAGLE – given to the individual recognized as "Manager of the Year."

In the past, THE EAGLE has been presented to the manager who delivered the best financial results. After consulting with many of you, we have decided to expand the rating criteria to more accurately reflect our corporate values and other business goals.

The criteria for THE EAGLE award will now consist of three equally-weighted measurements:

1. **Customer Satisfaction** – based on your department's customer satisfaction survey results.

2. **Employee Satisfaction** – based on your department's internal employee satisfaction survey.

3. **Financial Results** – based on your department's results as compared to the business plan.

THE EAGLE will be awarded to the manager who is best able to balance the priorities of our business: developing our people, taking care of our customers, and being profitable.

Thank you for your commitment and dedication to excellence.

Employee conversation around "the proverbial water cooler" ...

"Did you hear that Carlos turned in his notice. He's leaving in two weeks."

"You're kiddin' me!"

"No ... it's for real. He told me himself."

"What happened? Did he screw up?"

"Nope. Carlos is a great worker. This was his idea."

"But I thought he liked it here. And it sure seemed to me that he had a decent relationship with his boss."

"I thought so too – until I talked to him after work a couple of days ago. You know Carlos isn't the kind to moan or complain. But I got him to open up, and I found out that things weren't as rosy as they seemed. He's had a serious problem with his boss, Chris, for a while.

"It's about the way she continually '*delegates*' work to him. Actually, it's how she *doesn't* delegate that's got him walkin'."

"I'm not sure I understand."

"Apparently she has a pretty consistent habit of giving assignments and calling it delegation."

"That doesn't seem like such a big problem. Bosses give assignments all the time. Who cares what she calls it?"

"It's not what she calls it that's the problem. It's that she dumps the responsibility for doing the work and getting results on people, but keeps the authority and decision making power to herself. Basically, she calls all the shots and holds people accountable for the outcomes. Carlos is too sharp to always have to do things someone else's way – especially when other ways might make more sense."

"Did he try talking to her about it?"

"A bunch of times. She apparently told him that she appreciated his input, but making the calls was her responsibility."

"Man, that's too bad. Carlos has a lot of talent. I'm gonna miss him."

"We all will. But the one who's gonna feel the loss most is Chris. She's the big loser here."

E-mail sent to a recently promoted co-worker ...

Date: Today, 11:20 AM
From: me@stillhere.com
To: jeri@newjob.biz
Subject: WE MISS YA AROUND HERE!

Attach:

Hi, Jeri. How are things going in your division? You certainly deserved your promotion – but we REALLY miss you here. We're having a decent year ... almost in spite of ourselves. We could be doing a lot better, but sometimes it feels like we're on a treadmill: running real hard but not going very far.

Steve recently hired yet another person to take your place. This is the third person that he's brought in as your replacement in the last nine months. (Bet you didn't realize that you are irreplaceable, did you?) I don't know why Steve can't figure it out. If he would take his time and find the right person – instead of hiring people who barely pass the "can you fog a mirror" test – we'd all be better off.

He interviews a couple of people and settles for the one that "Steve the Miracle Worker" thinks he can develop. As soon as they come on board, it's obvious that they don't have the skills to be successful ... and he doesn't really have the time to work with them. Obviously, he never asks my opinion before he offers the job. Of course, what do I know – I've only been here five years. Ha! I would have told him to keep looking. We can handle things until he finds the right person.

It's frustrating (and more work for everybody) to break in a new person every few months. I can't see myself investing much time in Steve's next hire until I'm convinced that he or she is gonna be around a while.

Anyway, can you tell I really miss you being on our team? Let me know how things are going when you get a chance.

Take care.

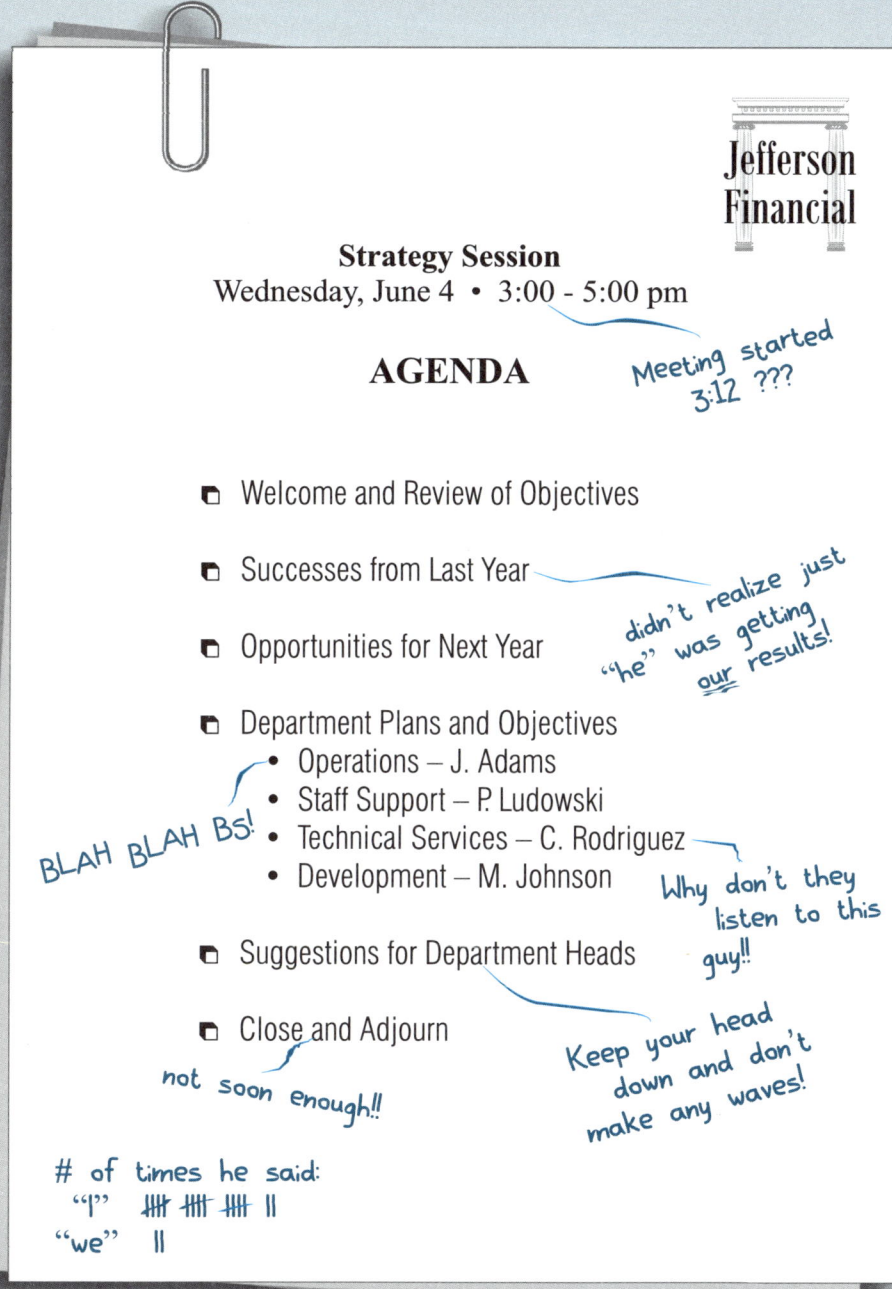

An employee's self-commendation – written only half in jest ...

Dear Me:

Seems like it's been a long time since the boss has seen fit to thank and recognize me for the good work that I do. And it's been even longer than that since I got any type of written commendation. I guess if I want one, I have to write it myself. So here it is.

I appreciate myself and everything I do around here. Although I do have my moments, I'm not one of those flash-in-the-pan superstars who get all the attention. No, I'm just a solid, reliable employee who, day in and day out, does my job well – without causing much fuss or bother. Guess that's why I'm so often invisible when it comes to management praise. Well, I'm not invisible to me, and I thank me for being one of the backbones of this business. And that's not all.

I thank me for showing up a little early, staying a little late, and occasionally working on a weekend to make sure the work gets done. I thank me for rarely causing problems for my boss or co-workers. I thank me for only having to be told once what needs to be done.

I rarely miss deadlines. I'm rarely off sick. And I pretty much always follow the rules. For all those things, and a lot more, I thank me.

Finally, thanks for noticing, thanks for appreciating, and most important, thanks for caring. If I ever get to be a boss, I promise me that I won't take all the other me's out there for granted ... and that I'll make a special effort to regularly say "Thank YOU."

Thanks again,

First of three e-mails sent home by a traveling spouse ...

Date: Today, 9:12 PM
From: spouse@ontheroad.com
To: honey@home.net
Subject: I'M HERE

Attach:

Hi Hon. I made it to the hotel. Had a good trip with no travel surprises! I miss you already.

I'm really kinda pumped about this meeting. I've already run into people that I haven't seen in years. It's funny how you take for granted the talent that we have in this company until we all get together for meetings like this. It may sound corny, but I'm really proud to be a part of this team! And everybody I've talked to is expecting a great meeting.

You remember me telling you about Kelly from Seattle? She was profiled in the corporate newsletter for setting all the sales records last year. Well, today I shared the shuttle van with her. What a dynamo! I'm looking forward to "picking her brain" during the next few days. When I checked in and received the meeting packet, I saw that Kelly is scheduled to present her success plan on Thursday. That should be great! I wonder why they waited until the last day to put our best sales person on the agenda? I think that we should start with her real-world success and end with the "paid political announcements." Oh, well. They didn't ask me what I wanted to get out of the meeting ... and they must have their reasons.

Some of the "big wigs" from corporate will be presenting tomorrow. It looks to be a pretty full day. Outside of being away from you, I'm excited to be here! This is a great time to get re-energized and pick up some new ideas that I can use when I get back.

It feels funny e-mailing you. But because of our schedules and different time zones, this is how we'll have to "talk" while I am gone. Will let you know how things are going tomorrow. Love ya!

Second e-mail sent home by traveling spouse ...

Date: Today, 10:18 PM
From: spouse@ontheroad.com
To: honey@home.net
Subject: TODAY

Attach:

Hi Sweetheart. Got your e-mail. I miss you too ... and I'm glad all is well there.

We had a less-than-stellar day here. Mr. Smith, the VP of Strategic Planning, kicked off the meeting. We were supposed to start at 9 AM, but he was late and we didn't get going until 9:30. His presentation was about how people are the most important assets in our company, yet he had over 100 of us waiting for him to show up. On top of that, his "one hour" presentation ran almost two hours, his visuals were poor, and he was rather preachy. Not a great start. Definitely not a good example to follow.

Next came our HR Director who spent a couple of hours telling us things most everyone already knew (or should have known). She could have sent us a two-page memo, before the meeting, to cover that material. Not the best use of our time.

Following lunch, things went from bad to worse ... we started late again. The new Information Technology Manager finally began his presentation by introducing a new performance data tracking and reporting process – from right out of the blue. No one had a clue a change was coming. And no one I talked to had a chance to input the process to make sure we end up with intelligence we can use. People are livid. So, instead of having the networking idea exchange tonight, we're breaking into teams to see if we can straighten this out. We have to come back tomorrow and present our recommendations. This better not take up any time allocated to the business development strategy sessions on tomorrow's schedule or I'll be livid too. I wonder how much money we're spending on this?

Oh well, the meeting should end on a high note, tomorrow, with Kelley giving us her customer service techniques and sales tips. That's something to look forward to.

Trying to stay positive. Miss you lots ... see you soon.

Third e-mail sent home by traveling spouse ...

Date: Today, 10:22 PM
From: spouse@ontheroad.com
To: honey@home.net
Subject: REPORT FROM THE ROAD

Attach:

Hi. There's a huge flight delay. Tried calling you but you must have been out. Since I have a bunch of time on my hands, I figured I'd send one last e-mail.

Can't wait to get home! This meeting was a major disappointment! I came with high expectations that I'd get energized, learn where the company is heading, and pick up ideas for doing my job better – I'm leaving frustrated and feeling like I am running on empty.

We spent the majority of today reworking that new IT data tracking and reporting process. And after all that, we wound up agreeing NOT to change the existing system. We spent almost a full day getting back to where we were before the meeting started! If they just would have really thought through the new manager's proposal – and asked for <u>our</u> input – we could have saved a lot of time and bad feelings.

To top it off, Kelly was asked to merely "summarize" what she had planned to say. Because of the time crunch, they promised to video tape her full presentation "at a later date" and send us all a copy of her success secrets. So now we have to wait a lot longer to get important information we can use. I don't understand this at all.

I think that most of the group is leaving disappointed, like me. However, since no one asked us what we expected or needed, maybe we shouldn't be surprised. And it's not the first time we've had this kind of "event." Still, I'm bummed out. In all honesty, my confidence in the leadership of the company isn't what it used to be. How can they squander resources like this but still hold us accountable for efficiency elsewhere. Maybe it is time for me to start looking for other opportunities.

Definitely looking forward to seeing you tonight – whenever I get in.

`Leadership survey results - A memo from the CEO ...`

MEMORANDUM

TO: All Managers, Supervisors, and Team Leaders
FROM: M. C. Jackson - Chief Executive Officer
SUBJECT: **Leadership Survey Executive Summary**

Attached you'll find the Executive Summary of our most recent Leadership Survey. You will receive more detailed results data in the complete survey package currently being compiled.

As you know, we conduct this type of survey every few years. It's important for us to receive feedback from employees on how we're doing as leaders. But even more important than collecting feedback is ACTING on the responses we receive. Otherwise, we're wasting peoples' time and creating false expectations. And it's here that I have a serious concern.

I *am* pleased with the "strength zones" that the survey identified. And we all need to constantly look for ways to maximize those things that we do well. But, just as with the survey conducted two years ago, we in leadership roles have received low marks regarding "people skills." Apparently, we've not done an adequate job of acting on the key learning from the last survey. We can't allow that to happen again. Therefore, I'll expect that each level of management will develop, and submit to their respective department heads, <u>specific action plans</u> for improving the way we manage and interact with our co-workers.

We owe this to our employees ... we owe this to ourselves!

Leadership survey results - The Attachment
(Executive Summary) ...

EXECUTIVE SUMMARY
Most Recent Leadership Survey

156 surveys were distributed to employees.
121 surveys were completed and returned.

General Response Patterns:

Organizational leadership scored well (identified strengths) in technical, customer-related, and "business-side" categories. Organizational leadership scored poorly (identified developmental opportunities) in interpersonal, performance management, and "people-side" categories.

Three Survey Items Receiving Highest Scores Overall:

- My manager possesses the technical skills necessary to perform all parts of his/her job effectively.
- My manager demonstrates a commitment to high levels of quality in the products and services we provide.
- My manager demonstrates a strong commitment to customers and customer service.

Three Survey Items Receiving Lowest Scores Overall:

- My manager provides me with the information I need to do my job effectively and feel like a member of the team.
- My manager addresses employee performance problems in a timely and effective manner.
- My manager encourages intelligent risk taking and views failures as opportunities to learn and grow.

From the "Letters to the Editor" section of the in-house newsletter ...

What about us?

Dear Editor,

I just returned from a luncheon for one of our retiring employees. It was especially nice and well deserved.

The honoree had dedicated 27 years to helping us become successful. Our CEO said some really nice things and gave the employee a beautiful watch. The best part for me was getting to know many of my co-workers in this casual setting.

The ceremony was great. But, after thinking more about it, I began wondering why it takes someone leaving before they are truly recognized for their contributions to our organization? Waiting until someone retires or resigns – and then trying to make him or her feel good about working here – doesn't make much sense to me.

What about those of us who have many more years before our careers end? We do a good job NOW! Why wait until a retirement for upper management to "mix with the workers" and eat lunch with us? Why is it we can't celebrate our many achievements *today* instead of waiting for years? Why not get together without the need for formal speeches on the agenda?

Our organization does a lot of things extremely well, and I'm proud to work here. Of course, celebrating the past with a dedicated retiring employee is an important tradition – one that we should continue. I just feel that we also need much more recognition of achievement in the present.

Anonymous

E-mail an employee typed out of frustration and then deleted before sending ...

Date: Today, 2:12 PM
From: frustratedme@here.badbiz
To: inconsiderateboss@here.badbiz
Subject: THANKS FOR NOTHING!

Attach: myresignation(Iwish).doc [18.6 KB]

Dear Boss:

I just wanted to thank you for another meeting that wasted everyone's time and accomplished nothing.

These meetings have been reduced to major league CYA events where "just get by" performers win, and the folks carrying the weight – the people who really care about this organization – are the losers.

You need to get out of your corner office and start listening – to customers ... and to employees. Learn for yourself what's REALLY happening in this organization before it's too late!

Someone who truly cares.

From a joint manager/employee training class:
"The T-shirt Exercise" ...

More restroom graffiti ...

the only place we have power around here is **in here!**

`Voice mail left on the "ethics hotline" ...`

"Ya know, I think it's great that we have an ethics program. But I've gotta tell you ... it's never gonna work as long as people are afraid to bring up issues.

There's a 'don't ruffle any feathers' attitude here – at least there is in *my* department. And unless you get that fixed, your ethics program – actually OUR ethics program – will be a joke. I don't want that to happen.

I hope someone there is *really* listening."

A week in the life of a manager who "walks the talk" ...

	MONDAY	TUESDAY	WEDNESDAY
7:00	*in early – visit with night shift*	7:00	7:00
8:00	*Marcus back from vacation – update him on what's happened*	8:00 *Effective Listening class – room 201 8:30 – 10*	8:00 *Kim's birthday – drop off card*
9:00		9:00	9:00
10:00		10:00 *f/u status mtg. on Margaret's project (ask about her son's swim meet)*	10:00 *Select team member to help with new-hire interviews*
11:00	*write commendation letter to Sam for perfect attendance*	11:00	11:00
12:00		12:00 *take Scott to lunch – 3 year anniversary with company*	12:00
1:00		1:00	1:00 *Monthly mentoring meeting with Linda*
2:00		2:00 *Meeting – get staff input on new equip. purchases*	2:00
3:00	*update staff on Sr. mgmt. meeting results*	3:00 *pre-perf. review meeting with Gabe to collect her input*	3:00 *help with order processing – Stuart on vacation day*
4:00	*performance discussion with Gene*	4:00	4:00
5:00		5:00	5:00
6:00	*stop at drugstore on way home – buy recognition cards*	6:00 *stay late – visit with swing shift*	6:00

-32-

THURSDAY	FRIDAY	SATURDAY
7:00	7:00	7:00
8:00	8:00	8:00 *visit with weekend crew - bring donuts*
9:00 *mtg. with Joan to discuss her personal development plans*	9:00 *teach values class at new-hire orient 8:30-10 room 206*	9:00
10:00	10:00	10:00 *Jennifer's soccer game*
11:00 *Coaching session with Fred*	11:00 *catch up on industry journal reading.*	11:00
12:00	12:00 *project completion celebration - order pizza*	12:00
1:00 *select employee to represent us at next month's conference*	1:00	1:00
2:00 *get out and chat with folks "how's it going?"*	2:00 *review team recommendations on new reporting process*	2:00
3:00	3:00 *team mtg: review this week - plan next week*	3:00
4:00 *"open door" meeting with Todd re: his scheduling concern*	4:00 *write/distribute recognition cards*	4:00
5:00	5:00	5:00
6:00	6:00	6:00

The resignation - Part 1 of 4: Resignation letter from Terri ...

August 24

Todd Washington
Manager
ACME Industries

Dear Todd,

Please accept this letter as my official notice of resignation, effective in two weeks.

I have enjoyed working with you for the past seven years. I have been offered a job with another organization that I feel will provide me with greater long-term opportunities.

Thank you for your leadership and guidance. I wish you and your team great success.

Sincerely,

Terri Collins

Terri Collins

The resignation - Part 2 of 4: Memo from manager to his boss explaining why Terri resigned ...

INNER-OFFICE COMMUNICATION

To: J. Garrett, Vice President
From: Todd Washington, Manager
Subject: Terri Collins' Resignation

Today I received Terri Collins' resignation letter.

As you know, Terri has been an outstanding, loyal employee for over seven years. The resignation came as a total surprise.

The reason Terri is leaving is because she perceives that she has a greater opportunity for advancement at XYZ Company. They must have enticed her with a lot more money because when I offered to increase her pay by 10%, she said she wasn't interested. I think they have also promised her an opportunity to move into management within the next two years.

She has convinced herself that the opportunities are greater at XYZ – and the money is probably much better.

The bottom line is that I think that she just wanted a change.

Todd

Todd Washington

The resignation - Part 3 of 4: Summary of Terri's
exit interview conducted by Human Resources ...

ACME INDUSTRIES EXIT INTERVIEW

Name   Terri Collins

What % increase in pay will you receive in new job?	5%
Will you receive a change in title?	No
Will you have a change in responsibility?	No

What influenced your decision to leave our company?
(Rate 1 = no influence to 5 = very influential)

Personal Issues:
- Childcare — 1
- Spouse Transfer — 1
- Personal Health — 1

Work-Related Issues:
- Compensation — 3
- Work Environment — 2
- Career Opportunities — 3

Please rate the following: (excellent, good, fair, poor)
- Health Benefits — excellent
- Leadership — fair/poor
- Overall Experience — fair

Comments from employee: None

Comments from Human Resources: <u>We are losing a good employee. It appears that the main reason she is leaving our company is because of a 5% increase in pay. There may be additional reasons, but she would not go into further detail.</u>

Would you recommend re-hiring this employee?   Yes

The resignation – Part 4 of 4: Orientation exercise Terri completed on first day at new company ...

Welcome to XYZ Company! We're excited that you've chosen to join our team! We feel it's important to understand why talented people, like you, leave their previous employer and come to work for us. Please take a few minutes to complete this anonymous survey.

Please rate the following factors – indicating how important each was in your decision to leave your previous employer. (1 = not important at all, 3 = some importance, 5 = very important)

Factor: Rating:

1. Pay/Benefits   2
   Comments: *The pay was ok. They did offer me a raise when I resigned, but compensation was not the reason that I left.*

2. Working Conditions   1
   Comments: *I enjoyed working with my co-workers. We had a pretty good team in spite of our manager. For the most part, I was provided the tools and training I needed to do my job.*

3. Opportunity to Learn, Grow, and Contribute   4
   Comments: *Growth opportunities were for the "politicians." The good, hard-working people were often ignored. Most of my co-workers could have done much more if given the opportunity and the encouragement.*

4. Management Support   5
   Comments: *I did not fully trust my manager. He talked about integrity a lot more than he practiced it. In addition, I received very little recognition, encouragement, coaching, or professional development.*

What can XYZ learn from your experience with your previous employer?
Take care of your people and they will take care of the business. My previous manager only showed interest in me when he needed something. He was clueless ... and now I'm here!

Results of employee training program table group exercise ...

Top Three Negative Organizational Behaviors

#1 Leaders who don't "walk the talk"

#2 People who don't pull their weight!

#3 Hiring and promoting supervisors who have good technical skills but poor "people practices"

Department bulletin board - from a low-performance organization ...

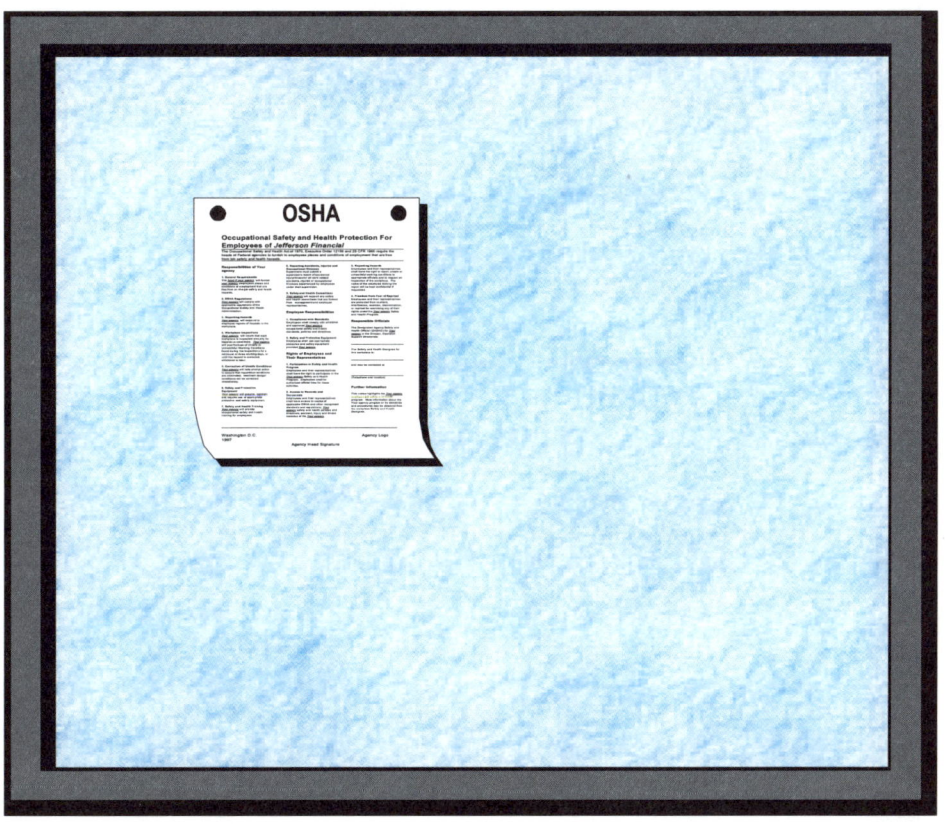

Department bulletin board - from a HIGH-performance organization ...

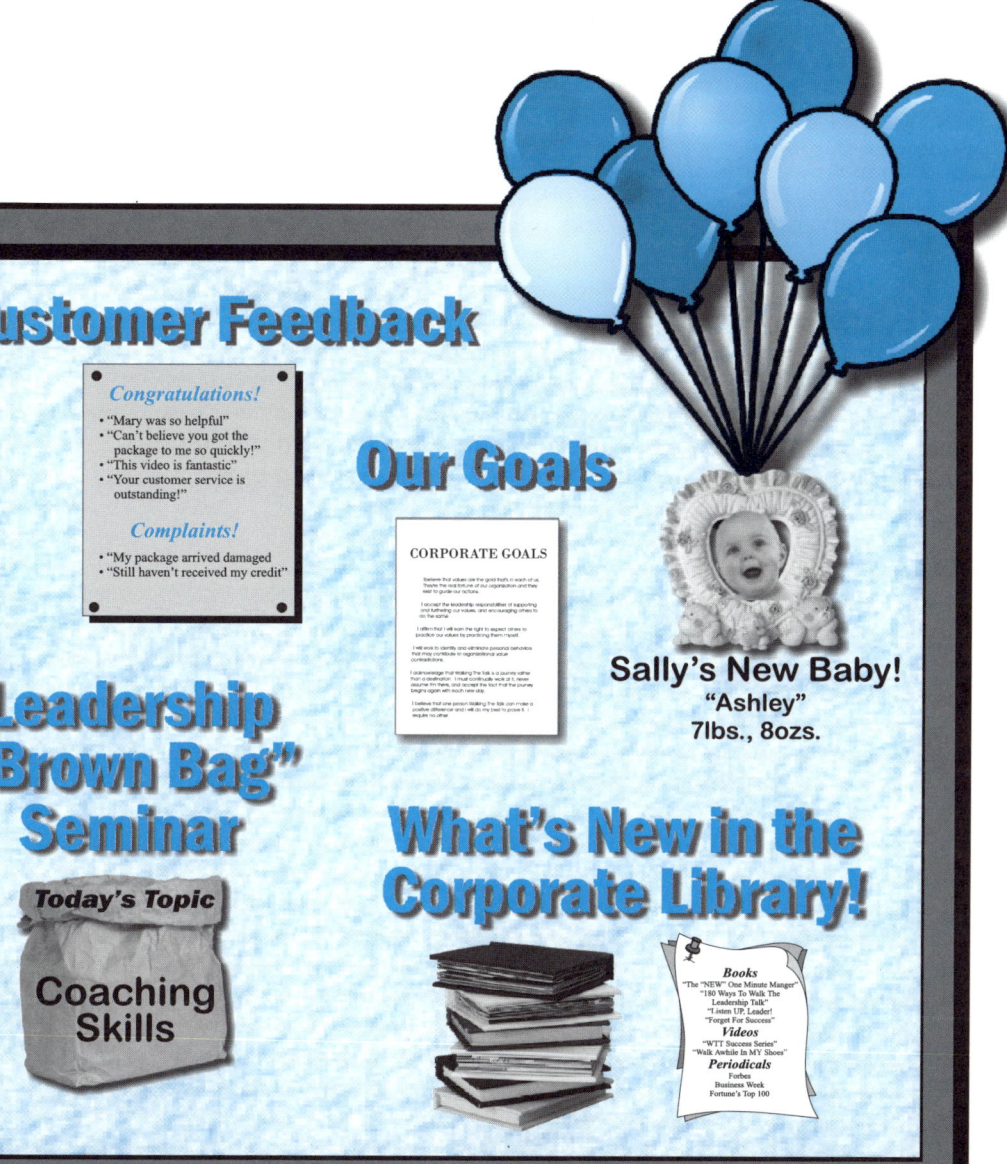

Last four speech note cards left on podium by retiring company CEO, April 2037 ...

39.

... And in conclusion, as I look back on my career – the highs and the lows, the tough times and the good times – I often think of my first manager (insert your name).

Here I was, fresh out of school – loaded with ambitious energy and optimism, but as green as they come.

I was, however, extremely fortunate to begin my career working for (your first name). I'm not sure I realized then how important this individual would be in shaping the perspectives I would have throughout my career.

40.

(Your name) was a great role model as well as a dedicated teacher and coach. As I move into retirement – having attained some measure of success – I realize the profound impact this individual had on me both professionally and personally.

Besides exhibiting high integrity, (your first name) took the time to mentor me – helping to identify my strengths and how I could use them to the fullest capacity.

(Your first name) also constructively pointed out my developmental opportunities and coached me to improve those weaknesses.

41.

Working for (your first name), I learned the value of recognition, the importance of a positive attitude, and the true meaning of ethics, integrity, and values-based business practices. As I look back on my early working experiences, I can tell you – without question – (your first name) was the single-most important contributor to my very satisfying career.

So my message to you supervisors, managers, team leaders – and yes, company executives – is to recognize the importance of your responsibilities as teachers, mentors, and role models. The long-term success of this organization will be determined by how well you help others learn, grow, and develop.

42.

As I finish the last day of my career, I recall what (your name) told me on my first day: "We judge ourselves by our intentions, but others judge us by our actions. And actions always speak louder than words." So, go forth, keep doing good things, and remember the wonderful lessons I've shared from MY role-model leader, (your name).

I truly appreciate the recognition you have given me here today. But more than that, I appreciate the opportunity I've had to serve as your chief executive for these past years.

Thank you ... and best wishes.

> Memo to file: Key learning from
> "MEMOS" To: Managers ...

TO: My ACTIVE File

FROM: (Insert Your Name)

DATE: Today

SUBJECT: **Key Learning From "MEMOS" To: Managers**

This handbook is jam-packed with important information. Perhaps the most significant take-away is that there are leadership lessons, to be absorbed, all around me – I just need to keep my eyes (and ears) open and pay attention. I've also come to realize that those many lessons are meaningful only if I actually USE them to become a better leader.

Specifically, I've learned that I need to ...

- Recognize the efforts and contributions of those I work with, and celebrate their successes;

- Involve employees in all aspects of our operation by asking for their input and ideas on what we do and how we do it;

- Help my people develop by providing training and guidance, and by sharing my knowledge and expertise through active coaching and mentoring;

- Delegate authority along with responsibility;

- Hire the right people and hold them accountable for carrying their share of the load;

- Clarify my expectations and keep people informed on how they're doing;

- Respect people's time by being prompt and prepared;

- Create a positive, enjoyable environment and exhibit contagious enthusiasm for our work, our customers, and our people;

- Keep people informed ... share the information that employees need to be successful and to feel like partners in achieving our business mission and goals;

- Support intelligent risk taking and view failures as learning opportunities;

- Deliver on my promises and commitments;

- Help my people balance their work and personal lives;

- Do my best to be accessible and available – especially when people need me;

- Be a role model for integrity and ethical, values-driven business practices;

- Show others what it means to WALK THE TALK;

And finally ...

- **Continue to read, learn from, and APPLY the *"Memos To Managers"* that are sent to me every day ... in so many different ways.**

Build Leadership Skills!

Since 1977, The WALK THE TALK Company has helped individuals build the skills and confidence they need to be effective leaders ... and helped organizations develop a culture of ethics and values-based business practices. And we're ready to do the same for YOU!

Like to learn about our ...
- Keynote and Conference Presentations
- Leadership Development Training
- Train-The-Trainer Resources
- "How To" Handbooks

and much more?

Contact The WALK THE TALK Professional Services team at
1.888.822.9255
or e-mail us at
solutions@walkthetalk.com.

The Authors

David Cottrell, President and CEO of CornerStone Leadership Institute, is an internationally known leadership consultant, educator, and speaker. He has authored eight publications, including two popular WALK THE TALK handbooks: *Listen Up, Leader!* and *The Manager's Coaching Handbook.*

Eric Harvey, a world-renowned author and business educator, is president of The WALK THE TALK Company. His 30-plus years of professional experience are reflected in fifteen highly acclaimed books, including the best-selling *WALK THE TALK...And Get The Results You Want* and *180 Ways To Walk The Recognition Talk.*

Four easy ways to order
"MEMOS" To: Managers

PHONE
Call **1.888.822.9255** toll free or 972.243.8863
8:30 a.m. to 5 p.m. Central, Monday through Friday

WEBSITE
Visit us on-line 24 hours a day at **www.walkthetalk.com**

OR, complete the order form on the back and return it by either:

MAIL
The WALK THE TALK Co.
2925 LBJ Freeway, Suite 201
Dallas, Texas 75234

FAX
972.243.0815

Looking for more Management Development resources? We've got plenty!

Check out ALL of our popular, high-impact publications in one convenient package ... and save money.

When you place your order, include a

Get **16** handbooks

plus
The best-selling hardback
Walk The Talk ... And Get The Results You Want

$119.95
(retail value $181.15)

FREE Do-It-Yourself Training!
Looking for training ideas on Management Development that you can use <u>immediately</u>?
Check out our free "Do-It-Yourself Training" resources at
www.walkthetalk.com.

ORDER FORM

*Have questions? Need assistance? Call **1.888.822.9255***

"MEMOS" To: Managers

1-99 – $9.95 each
100-499 – $9.45 each
500-4,999 – $8.95 each
5,000+ – call

Copies _____
Book Total $ _____

Deluxe Leadership Library
(shown on previous page)

$119.95 each

Libraries _____
Library Total $ _____

Book Total + Library Total $ _____ (A)

*Shipping and Handling +$ _____
(Continental U.S. – $4.00 plus 6% of <u>line (A)</u> above)

Subtotal $ _____

Texas Only – Sales Tax (8.25% of Subtotal) +$ _____

TOTAL $ _____

*SHIPPING & HANDLING:

*Outside the continental U.S., please call 972.243.8863.
Orders shipped ground delivery to be received in 7-10 business days.
Priority shipping available – call 1.888.822.9255.*

☐ **YES,** I would like to learn more about WALK THE TALK® Keynotes, Workshops, Consulting, and Training Services. Please contact me via: ☐ phone ☐ e-mail.

Name (MR/MRS/MS) _____

Title _____

Organization _____

Street Address _____
(do not use P.O. Box)

City _____ State _____ Zip _____ Country _____

Phone (required to process order) ( ) _____ Ext. _____

Fax ( ) _____ e-mail _____

Purchase Order Number (if applicable) _____

☐ MasterCard ☐ VISA ☐ American Express ☐ Check or Money Order Enclosed *(Payable to: The WALK THE TALK Co.)* ☐ **My order is over $250** Please invoice.

Account Number _____ Expiration Date _____
(month/year)

Signature _____

Prices effective July 1, 2002 are subject to change without notice. Orders payable in U.S. dollars only. Orders outside U.S. and Canada must be prepaid by credit card or check drawn on a U.S. bank. Orders under $250 must be prepaid by credit card, check, or money order. Restocking fee on returns within 30 days of original receipt.

THANK YOU FOR YOUR ORDER.